Professional Interior Design

Professional Interior Design

◆

a career guide

ASID Illinois; Jason A Znoy

iUniverse, Inc.

New York Lincoln Shanghai

Professional Interior Design
a career guide

iUniverse, Inc.

For information address:
iUniverse, Inc.
2021 Pine Lake Road, Suite 100
Lincoln, NE 68512
www.iuniverse.com

This book is for educational and informational purposes only. ASID Illinois does not endorse any individual educational institution or professional organization.

ISBN: 0-595-31909-2

Printed in the United States of America

Contents

Introduction

We hope that this book will give the reader a good, solid understanding of the industry as you begin your job search. In compiling this handbook, we have culled information from various references, including statements by other professional designers from their personal experiences. The ideas and recommendations presented here are generally accepted in the industry. This does not mean that they are hard and fast rules. This book is only intended as a guideline to help lead you on your way to a successful career.

Ultimately, we have found that there is no substitute for practice and experience. Your first job interviews will confirm this premise. The painstaking time and effort that you will put into your own job search and career development will result in a rewarding career.

1

Design Basics

GENERAL DESIGN

Designers are people with a basic desire to create. They combine practical knowledge with artistic ability to turn abstract ideas into formal designs for the merchandise we buy, the clothes we wear, the publications we read, and the living and office space we inhabit. Designers usually specialize in a particular area of design, such as automobiles, industrial or medical equipment; interiors of homes or office buildings; merchandise displays; or movie, television and theater sets. Through experience and education they receive their title of engineer, architect, interior designer, fashion designer or textile specialists. But they are always designers.

INTERIOR DESIGN HISTORY

Interior design is an identified career option. But before there were 'interior designers,' there were interior decorators. The term interior decorator has been in use since the mid-19th century, its definition having taken a variety of turns. Anyone involved with any of the elements of the interiors can call themselves a decorator, whether a wallpaper hanger or a mural painter.

Through college-level programs, professional exams, title acts and profession acts, a new field called "interior design" has been established and is recognized by state regulatory boards with levels of creditability; professional status being the end result.

THE PROFESSION

Professional interior designers plan the space and furnish the interiors of private homes, public buildings, and business facilities, such as offices, restaurants, retail establishments, hospitals, hotels, and theaters. They also plan the interiors when existing structures are renovated or expanded.

The profession can be divided into two distinct specialties: residential and non-residential/contract design. Residential design focuses on private dwellings, apartments, condos, single family dwellings and may include RVs, houseboats and other related vacational transportation. Non-residential design focuses on offices, restaurants, hotels, retail, institutional and government spaces.

Definition of a Professional Interior Designer

The professional interior designer is qualified by education, experience, and examination to enhance the function and quality of interior spaces for the purpose of improving the quality of life, increasing productivity, and protecting the health, safety, and welfare of the public.

The professional interior designer:

Analyzes client's needs, goals, and life safety requirements;

Integrates findings with knowledge of interior design;

Formulates preliminary design concepts that are aesthetic, appropriate, and functional, and in accordance with codes and standards;

Develops and presents final design recommendations through appropriate presentation media;

Prepares working drawings and specifications for non-load bearing interior construction, reflected ceiling plans, lighting, interior detailing, materials, finishes, space planning, furnishings, fixtures, and equipment in compliance with universal accessibility guidelines and all applicable codes;

Collaborates with professional services of other licensed practitioners in the technical areas of mechanical, electrical, and load-bearing design as required for regulatory approval;

Prepares and administers bids and contract documents as the client's agent;

Reviews and evaluates design solutions during implementation and upon completion.

Many interior designers specialize. For example, some may concentrate in residential design, and others may further specialize by focusing on particular rooms, such as kitchens and baths or using a philosophy such as sustainable design. With a client's tastes, needs, budget and specialized information in mind interior designers prepare drawings and specifications for non-load bearing interior construction, furnishings, lighting and finishes.

Increasingly, designers use computers to plan layouts and prepare documents for construction. Interior designers also design lighting and architectural details, such as crown molding, built-in bookshelves, cabinetry, furniture, floor coverings and fabrics. Designed spaces must conform to federal, state and local laws, including building codes. Designs must meet accessibility standards for the disabled and elderly, per the Americans with Disabilities Act.

In the day-to-day experiences, the professional interior designer works off of scaled drawings of existing spaces and a list of client requirements to organize a structured space. The designer uses design elements and principles including lighting, textiles, furniture, color, floor finishes and wall effects to meet the requirements from the client, while always keeping in mind the regulations set by local building codes and issues that affect health and safety. In the end, the final product will be a plan that fulfills the clients needs and wishes while being on budget.

The first step in developing a new design or altering an existing one is to determine the needs of the client, the ultimate function for which the design is intended.

Designers then prepare sketches, by hand or with the aid of a computer, to illustrate the vision for the design. After consulting with the client, designers create detailed interiors using drawings, a structural model, computer simulations or a full-scale prototype. Many designers increasingly are using computer-aided design (CAD) tools to create and better visualize the final product. Computer models allow greater ease and flexibility in exploring a greater number of design alternatives, thus reducing design costs and cutting the time it takes to deliver a product to market.

Designers sometime supervise assistants who carry out their creations. Designers who run their own business also may devote a considerable amount of time to developing new business contacts, reviewing equipment and space needs, and performing administrative tasks such as reviewing catalogs and ordering samples.

Working conditions and places of employment vary. Designers employed by manufacturing establishments, large corporations or design firms generally work regular hours. Self-employed designers tend to work longer hours and often from home.

Designers who work on contract, or per job basis, frequently adjust their workday to suit their clients' schedules; meeting with clients during evening or weekend hours when necessary. Designers may transact business in their own offices or studio, in a client's home or office, or they may travel to other locations such as showrooms, design centers, a client's project site and manufacturing facilities. Most designers charge on a per hour basis for services rendered. Any goods sold are sold at cost or with a mark-up. With the increased use of computers in the workplace and the advent of the Internet, more designers conduct business, research design alternatives and purchase goods electronically.

TRAINING AND ADVANCEMENT

Creativity is crucial in all design occupations. People in this field must have a strong sense of the esthetic: an eye for color and detail, a sense of balance and proportion and an appreciation for beauty. Despite the advancement of computer-aided design, sketching ability remains an important advantage in most types of design. A good portfolio, a collection of examples of a person's best work, often is the deciding factor in getting a job. A degree is necessary for most entry-level design positions.

Interior design is subject to government regulation. According to the American Society for Interior Designers (ASID), 24 states and jurisdictions require interior designers to be licensed or registered. Passing the National Council for Interior Design Qualification (NCIDQ) examination is required for licensure, legally recognizing the interior design profession and registration. Because licensing is not mandatory in all states, membership in a professional association is an indication of an interior designer's qualifications and professional standing; and can aid in obtaining clients.

Formal training for some interior design professions also is available in two and three-year professional schools that award certificates or associate degrees in design. Graduates of 2-year programs normally qualify as assistants to designers. A bachelor's degree is granted at 4-year colleges and universities. The curriculum in these schools may include art and art history, principles of design, designing and sketching and specialized studies for each of the individual design disciplines, such as textiles, architectural drawing, computerized design, codes, materials and sources. A liberal arts education with courses in general education is recommended for designers who will be working with well educated and traveled clients. Because CAD is increasingly common, many employers expect new designers to be familiar with its use as a design tool. Interior designers use computers to create numerous versions of the built environment; images can be inserted, edited and replaced easily and without added cost, making it possible for a client to see and choose among several designs.

The Foundation for Interior Design Education Research (FIDER) accredits four-year interior design programs and schools. Currently, there are more than 136 accredited professional programs in the United States and Canada, primarily located in schools of art, architectural studies, department of human environmental sciences and single-subject colleges.

Individuals in the design field must be creative, imaginative, persistent, and able to communicate their ideas in writing, visually and verbally. Because personal tastes can change quickly, designers need to be well-read, open to new ideas and influences, and quick to react to changing trends. Problem-solving skills and the ability to work independently and under pressure are important traits. People in this field need self-discipline to start projects on their own, to budget their time and to meet deadlines and production schedules. Good business sense and sales ability also are important, especially for those who consult or run their own business.

Beginning designers usually receive on-the-job training, and normally need one to three years of training before they can advance to higher-level positions. Experienced designers in large firms may advance to chief designer, design department head or other supervisory positions. Some designers become adjunct teachers in design schools and colleges and universities. Many faculty members continue to consult privately or operate small design studios to complement their classroom activities. Some experienced designers open their own firms.

Despite projected faster-than-average employment growth, designers in this field are expected to face keen competition for available positions. Many talented individuals are attracted to careers as designers. Individuals with little or no formal education in design, as well as those who lack creativity and perseverance, will find it very difficult to establish and maintain a career in interior design.

The US Department of Labor expects the employment of designers to grow faster than the average for all other occupations through the year 2010. In addition to those that result from employment growth, many job openings will arise from the need to replace designers who leave the field.

2

Evaluating Your Education

ACCREDITATION

Accreditation is a process unique to the United States and Canada that replaces government regulation of education found in most other countries. It is a process of self-evaluation and peer review that promotes achievement of high academic standards, while making education more responsive to students and society's needs. Standards developed by interior design practitioners and educators and concern for continued growth and development are central to accreditation.

The Foundation for Interior Design Education Research (FIDER) accredits interior design programs in North America. FIDER is a specialized accreditation agency, accrediting interior design programs at colleges and universities. Its mission is to "lead the interior design profession to excellence by setting standards and accrediting academic programs."

The accrediting process begins with a comprehensive self-study by the program, followed by a series of evaluations and reviews by a FIDER visiting team, its evaluation committee, and finally the FIDER accreditation commission. The commission makes the final decision to award or deny accreditation. All evaluators are interior design practitioners and educators.

Though this accreditation students receive an education that is recognized by the interior design profession as meeting educational requirements for entry into the profession. In the future this factor may impact the right to practice in states with licensing or registering acts.

Through graduating from a FIDER-accredited program is not yet required to practice interior design, students can be confident that their program voluntarily placed itself before the scrutiny of the profession; investing time, energy, and money, to ensure that their graduates receive an education that meets the standards of the profession and will serve them now and into the future.

THE STANDARDS

This chapter is not meant to claim that FIDER is the end all of quality interior design programs nor is stating that programs not FIDER-accredited are not worthwhile. The standards set by FIDER are of a high caliber. Through accreditation, prospective students know that their college will have met a basic quality standard. All criteria used to measure programs may be used to also reference other programs for merit. The following is taken directly from FIDER's accreditation guidelines.

Standard 1: Curriculum Structure

The curriculum is structured to facilitate and advance student learning. The curriculum must follow a logical sequence. Course content must increase in degree of difficulty. Significant concepts must be interrelated and reinforced throughout the curriculum. Projects must demonstrate variety and complexity in type, size and scope.

The teaching and learning methods must incorporate the experience of team approaches to design solutions and experiences that provide interaction with multiple disciplines (for example, code specialists, engineers, architects, artists, behaviorists) representing a variety of points of view and perspectives on design problems.

The program must provide interaction with practicing professionals (for example, as jurors, project critics, guest lecturers, mentors), exposure to a variety of business cultures and organizational structures (for example, for-profit, non-profit, publicly or privately held, hierarchical, flat) and opportunities for design work experience (for example, internship, co-op, shadowing, or other experiences that familiarize students with the culture and environment of the professional studio and professional practice).

Standard 2: Professional Values

The program leads students to develop the attitudes, traits, and values of professional responsibility, accountability, and effectiveness. The program must incorporate learning experiences that address client and/or user needs and their responses to the interior environment. The program must present opportunities or experiences that address the value and importance of community or public service.

The program must provide learning experiences that address professional ethics and the role of ethics in interior design, consciousness of alternate points of view and appreciation of cultural diversity, the designer's ability to affect people and the environment and a global perspective and approach to thinking and problem solving.

The program must include learning experiences that incorporate critical, analytical, and strategic thinking, creative thinking (exhibit a variety of ideas, approaches, concepts with originality and elaboration), the ability to think visually and volumetrically, professional discipline (for example, time management, organizational skills) and active listening skills leading to effective interpretation of requirements (programming interviews, participatory critiques, role playing)

Standard 3: Design Fundamentals

Students have a foundation in the fundamentals of art and design, theories of design and human behavior, and discipline-related history.

Student work must demonstrate understanding of design fundamentals including design elements (for example, space, line, mass, shape, texture) and principles (for example, scale, proportion, balance, rhythm, emphasis, harmony, variety), color principles, theories, and systems (for example, additive and subtractive color; color-mixing; hue, value, and intensity; the relationship of light and color), theories of design and design composition (for example, functionalism, Gestalt) and principles of lighting design (for example, color, quality, sources, use).

Student work must demonstrate understanding of theories of human behavior and interior environments human factors (for example, ergonomics, anthropometrics) and the relationship between human behavior and the built environment. Student work must demonstrate understanding of history including art, architecture, interiors and furnishings.

Standard 4: Interior Design

Students understand and apply the knowledge, skills, processes, and theories of interior design. Student work must follow a process and demonstrate the ability to apply 2-dimensional design elements and principles in interior design projects, apply 3-dimensional design elements and principles to the development of the spatial envelope (for example, volumes of space, visual continuity and balance, visual passages, interconnecting elements) and select and apply color in interior design projects.

Student work must demonstrate programming skills, including: problem identification, problem solving, identification of client and/or user needs and information gathering research and analysis (functional requirements, code research, etc.).

Student work must demonstrate competent schematic design and concept development skills, including concept statements, the ability to rapidly visualize concepts through sketching and space planning (adjacencies, circulation, and articulation and shaping of space).

Student work must demonstrate competent design development skills in selection of interior finishes and materials, detailed and developed layout of furniture, fixtures, and equipment, detailed and developed furniture selection, space plans, elevations, sketches, and study models, selection and application of luminaries and lighting sources, justifying design solutions relative to the goals and objectives of the project program and appropriate selection and application of decorative elements.

Student work must demonstrate competent skills in preparing drawings, schedules, and specifications as an integrated system of contract documents, appropriate to project size and scope and sufficiently extensive to show how design solutions and interior construction are related. These could include construction/demolition plans, power plans, lighting/reflected ceiling plans, finish plans, furniture, fixtures, and equipment plans, data/voice telecommunication plans, elevations, sections, and details, interior building specifications, furniture specifications, finish schedules, door schedules, etc. (The intent of this indicator is to demonstrate how contract documents are used as an integrated system. Documents should not be scattered across the curriculum, but neither do all examples need to be evidenced in a single project.)

Student work should demonstrate design development skills, including appropriate selection and application of art and accessories, the ability to design custom interior elements (for example, case goods, floor patterning, textiles), way finding methods and graphic identification, such as signage.

Standard 5: Communication

Students communicate effectively. Student work must demonstrate competence in drafting and lettering, both manual and computer-aided techniques, illustrative sketching and presentation of color, materials, and furnishings (for example, sample boards, collages, mock-ups, digital representations).

Students must express ideas clearly in oral presentations and critiques and communicate clearly in writing (using correct spelling, grammar, and syntax) in specifications, schedules, and contracts and other business-related documents such as project programs, concept statements, reports, research papers, resumes, and correspondence.

Student work should demonstrate the ability to render (for example, pencil, marker, or other manual media, or by computer—any medium that successfully communicates the design intent), draw in perspective, construct models, apply the metric system to design work and communicate through alternative presentation techniques (for example, audio, electronic, film, photography, slides, video).

Standard 6: Building Systems and Interior Materials

Students design within the context of building systems. Students use appropriate materials and products.

Students must demonstrate understanding that design solutions affect and are impacted by construction systems and methods (for example, wood-frame, steel-frame, masonry, concrete), power distribution systems, mechanical systems (HVAC, plumbing), energy management, data/voice telecommunications systems, lighting systems, ceiling systems, flooring systems (for example, raised, heated), security systems, acoustics and interface of work station furniture systems with building systems.

Student work must demonstrate that materials and products are appropriately selected and applied on the basis of their properties and performance criteria. Students must demonstrate knowledge of sources for materials and products. Students should demonstrate understanding of the concept of sustainable resources. Students should demonstrate knowledge of installation methods (for example, carpet, resilient flooring and wallcovering) and material maintenance requirements.

Standard 7: Regulations

Students apply the laws, codes, regulations, standards, and practices that protect the health, safety, and welfare of the public.

Student work must demonstrate understanding of the impact of fire and life safety principles compartmentalization (fire separation), movement (stairwells, corridors, exitways), detection (smoke/heat detectors and alarm systems) and suppression (sprinklers/fire hose cabinets).

Student work must demonstrate the appropriate application of codes, regulations, and standards (for example, American National Standards Institute, Construction Specifications Institute, Illuminating Engineering Society, National Building Code, Uniform Building Code), barrier-free design concepts (for example, Americans with Disabilities Act) and ergonomic and human factors data.

Students must demonstrate understanding of the impact on health and welfare of indoor air quality, noise and lighting. Student work must demonstrate understanding of universal design concepts and principles.

Standard 8: Business and Professional Practice

Students have a foundation in business and professional practice.

Students must demonstrate understanding of project management practices estimating (for example, project costs, fees), budget management, coordination (managing input from various members of the project team), time management, scheduling, and contract administration, information management (collecting and disseminating relevant project information), conflict resolution (facilitating solutions to conflicting objectives) and assessment processes (for example, post-occupancy evaluation, productivity, square-footage ratios).

Students must demonstrate knowledge of certification, licensing, and/or registration requirements and professional design organizations. Students should demonstrate understanding of basic business computer applications (for example, word processing, spreadsheets). Students should demonstrate knowledge of business processes (for example, marketing, strategic planning, and accounting procedures).

Standard 9: Faculty

Faculty members and other instructional personnel are qualified and adequate in number to implement program objectives.

Faculty members and other instructional personnel represent more than one professional point of view, design background, and experience, have academic and/ or professional experience appropriate to their areas of responsibility, participate in relevant professional and/or scholarly associations (for example, American Society of Interior Designers, Interior Designers of Canada, Interior Design Educators Council, International Interior Design Association), engage in scholarly research, practice, and/or creative activity leading to professional growth and the advancement of the profession and engage in continuing education.

A majority of faculty members and other instructional personnel with interior design studio supervision have earned a degree in interior design and have passed the complete National Council for Interior Design Qualification exam.

The number of faculty members and other instructional personnel is sufficient to implement program objectives.

Standard 10: Facilities

Program facilities and resources provide an environment to stimulate thought, motivate students, and promote the exchange of ideas. Instructional facilities and workspaces support program objectives and course goals. Program objectives and course goals are supported by the appropriate equipment (for example, computers, printers, plotters, projectors, monitors/VCRs). Spaces are available for collaborative activities, such as exhibitions, critique, display, and working in teams.

Students have convenient access to a comprehensive and current range of information about interior design and relevant disciplines (for example, bound volumes, periodicals, microfilm, video, slides, electronic) and product information (bound, electronic, or on-line) and samples.

Faculty members and other instructional personnel have facilities and equipment for course preparation, project evaluation, administrative activities, and/or conferences and sufficient technical and/or clerical support.

Standard 11: Administration

The administration of the program is clearly defined, provides appropriate program leadership, and supports the program. The program demonstrates accountability to the public through its published documents.

The administrative unit(s) in which the program is located support(s) program goals. Clear channels of communication exist between the program and departmental and/or administrative unit in which it is located. The coordinator, faculty members, and other instructional personnel collaborate in developing, implementing, and modifying the program.

The coordinator is a full-time faculty member qualified by education and experience to administer an interior design program and participates in the recruitment, evaluation, and retention of program faculty and instructional personnel.

The program provides clear, consistent, and reliable information to the public regarding admission policies, program philosophy, mission, and goals, course of study, academic quality and student achievement.

Standard 12: Assessment

Systematic and comprehensive assessment methods contribute to the program's ongoing development and improvement. The program uses input from various groups (for example, enrolled students, faculty members, employers, alumni, Advisory Board, local design organizations) in developing and implementing strategies for improvement. The program regularly monitors and evaluates professional placement of alumni.

In addition, it is important to acknowledge the ever-changing nature of the education required for a growing profession.

The responsibilities of the interior designer encompass all spaces within environments built for human habitation. Educational philosophies and goals should be applied in the development of a creative professional that can synthesize information, and analyze problems from many different perspectives.

OF NOTE

Institutions of higher learning constantly re-examine their goals and directions. New technologies affect the skills and knowledge required of interior designers. The best preparation for the future is an education that will enable graduates to adapt to a changing world. Adaptation to change requires that the graduate draw on history and on the experience of many cultures and apply the theories and methods of empirical investigation. A sound curriculum for professional interior design education must provide a balance between the broad cultural aspects of education, on the one hand, and the specialized practical content integral to the profession, on the other.

Programs must work within their individual institutions to offer the widest possible benefits to students. The stimulation and advice from a variety of subject areas of an institution are major advantages of postsecondary education.

To ensure excellence, interior design programs must maintain high standards of student and institutional performance, measuring the results against FIDER's established performance standards.

3

Getting the Job

INITIAL RESEARCH

Find out as much as you can on our prospective employers including its employees, clients, previous and current projects, financial situations and management philosophy. You can check a company's finances through the US Securities and Exchange Commission. Modern researchers have a miraculous tool: the Internet. There is such a wealth of information available to you on the Internet; though it is possible to find too much or unnecessary information

Decide on the type of job and geographic location.
Research possible companies websites for mission statements, service information, principal's background, and contact information.
Talk to people in the know, a.k.a. networking.
Check job listings.

THE RESUME

Your resume is the first contact with a potential employer. It is often the only chance you have to make any impression. The resume can be considered a marketing tool, an advertisement to sell you to that potential employer. The purpose of the resume is to make the employer want to meet you through your skills, experiences and accomplishments. You must remember that your resume is much different from a job application. A job application is about your jobs and your employment history. A resume is about you and your accomplishments. Your resume should never be more than two pages in length.

Your resume must be perfect. Make sure there are no typing errors or misspelled words. Use spellchecker, check it yourself, and have a friend check it. It is also highly suggested to contact associates in the field or in your professional organization to review your resume for feedback. This is your foot in the door; it must be flawless.

There are two basic types of resumes: chronological and functional.

A chronological resume presents work experience through a date-orientated format, listing the jobs held and describing their activities and accomplishments in paragraphs; containing the most recent position first. Divisions of a chronological resume include:

Name
Objective
Highlights
Relevant Experience

A functional resume presents your experience with the most important skills and then outlines a number of activities and accomplishments associated with each skill. This is the type most requested by employers. Divisions of a functional resume include:

Name
Objective
Summary of Qualifications
Relevant Skills
Employment History
Education
Community Service
Professional Organizations

You will need to assemble your educational and personal history to see which format best represents you. More often graduating students will follow the functional resume whereas professionals in the field, with some experience under their belt, will follow the chronological resume format. Remember, that everyone is different and each situation will need to be addressed individually.

THE DIVISIONS OF THE RESUME

Career Objective

This section can come under many titles: job objective, objective, career objective, career goal; but the purpose is always the same. This section tells the employer about you and how you can perform in the position. Your career objective focuses attention on your goal and aids in choosing the most important things to say in the remainer of the resume. To do this you will make a list of your strongest, and favorite, skills and abilities that are relevant to the job. It is often best to do this first because it will allow you to discover what type of position you want and are best suited; plus it will determine what to leave or take out of your resume to better sell yourself.

Work History

Write several accomplishments, approximately three to four from your work history to illustrate each skill that relates to the target job. Use the format of: problem, action and results. Then rephrase each accomplishment in a simple, yet powerful statement that emphasizes results that benefited your employer. Include action words near the beginning of each accomplishment. Make sure to mention specific, provable, successful results whenever possible. This also allows you to delete and thus not include activities you never want to do again so that you will not end up with a position you will not enjoy.

Make a list of previous jobs in chronological order: dates of employment, job titles, and employer. If large gaps occur include unpaid work and educations that fill gaps or shows skills for the job to provide a picture of stability. These jobs do not need to be described in detail. Omit brief jobs unless necessary to show development of skills. Another tactic to eliminate gaps is to round dates to the year, rather than the month. Older applicants may want to eliminate earlier jobs to reduce possibility of age discrimination.

Applicants with a diverse background may want to use a functional arrangement rather than a chronological. In chronological, action statements are placed under their appropriate job title. Functional arrangement lists action statements under a skill category.

Education

Make a list of training and education related to your job. Correspondence courses, apprenticeships, work-study programs, and relevant workshops including CEUs and conferences like NeoCon may be included in this section.

Academic credentials and degrees beyond high school should be included at this time. For training courses, just list the certificate earned. For uncompleted training, list every course taken related to the target job (this is usable for applicants still in school).

Action Verbs

acquainted	documented	organized
adapted	edited	originated
aided	elected	oversaw
allocated	enlisted	patented
analyzed	evaluated	persuaded
appraised	exceeded	pioneered
arranged	executed	planned
assembled	expanded	prepared
assessed	explained	presided
assisted	financed	processed
attained	formalized	produced
attended	formed	publicized
audited	fostered	published
augmented	founded	recorded
awarded	gathered	recruited
benchmarked	governed	reduced
built	hired	reengineered
collaborated	identified	reorganized
collected	implemented	represented
compiled	improved	reviewed
composed	increased	routed
conceived	initiated	saved
conceptualized	inspired	scheduled
conducted	instituted	selected
consulted	interpreted	sold
contacted	introduced	solicited
contributed	invented	spearheaded
coordinated	led	sponsored
counseled	maintained	staged
decreased	managed	started
demonstrated	marketed	supervised
designed	mediated	supported
detected	mentored	surveyed
determined	moderated	taught
devised	motivated	tested
discovered	negotiated	trained
disseminated	operated	updated
distributed	orchestrated	wrote

Professional Profile

This has been left until the end because it is not widely used, but can often be a powerful tool; especially for candidates with internships, travel abroad experiences and attendance in professional seminars. Referred to as summary of qualifications, highlights, professional profile, qualifications, etc.; this section highlights the most relevant strengths and features of experience. Make a brief, bulleted list of four or six key points that will make you look attractive and qualified to the employer. Place this section just below your job target. Examples include recognition, key skills, talents, special knowledge, and descriptions of your personal work style and attitude.

THE COVER LETTER

Your cover letter is the introduction to your resume. Many have the misconception that the cover letter should contain your qualifications for your prospective job position including details about you. This is absolutely untrue. The cover letter is only included to notify the receiver of the position you are interested and illustrate your research into the company. The resume is included to sell you, your background and abilities. Even though the resume is the most important element, the quality of the cover letter must not be compromised. It is helpful to have the cover letter on the same formatted letterhead as the resume, in case the two are separated.

A brief, well-written, to-the-point cover letter lures the recruiter into reviewing your resume and giving you a call. Three major mistakes to watch out for: vagueness, bad writing, unnecessary creativity and writing too much. A few points to remember:

1. Address your letter to an individual. If not possible, it is best to use a neutral yet formal greeting, such as "Dear Hiring Manager."

2. Show that you are familiar with the company by including how you can fit into their corporate identity or solve a current problem. The company's website is often useful to do such.

3. Include when and how you will be following up to illustrate a true interest. (Make sure to follow-up as stated)

4. Sign your letter by typing in your name. Include all contact information in the text of the letter and again in the signature line.

5. Proofread your letter. Mistakes in grammar and spelling are much more frequent in email, so be sure to check using both a spell-check program and manually through a hard copy.

6. Specify your interest in the subject line to make your resume stand out from the high volume of junk mail

7. Keep it brief. The hiring professional has many resumes to go through and too many words will discourage them from reading on.

8. Remember to attach your resume. Do not include unnecessary attachments like photos or backgrounds.

THE PORTFOLIO

Your portfolio should include your best work. You should not bring your entire portfolio to the interview, only the work that pertains to the position. Your portfolio should be a self-explanatory body of work. This self-sufficient portfolio will also help make your interview process run smoothly, especially when the portfolio needs to be sent by post or email.

Generally, your portfolio should include perspective/isometric drawings, renderings, photos of models and at least one consistent design set including:

Program
Concept Statement
Preliminary Design Sketches
Bubble Diagrams
Complete Drawing Set
1. Partition Plan
2. Furnishings Plan
3. Electrical Plan
4. Lighting Plan
5. Details and Custom Drawings

As they examine your portfolio, interviewers will be looking for different skills, depending on the position to be filled and the orientation of the firm. However, a strong portfolio should demonstrate a number of general skills and abilities. A concept statement, a concise written explanation of the project parameters, should be included for each project to orient the viewer to the design problem. Employers like to see the evolution of design from problem to solution, so you may include sketches exemplifying the process. These do not have to be professionally bound, but included.

The format of your portfolio is entirely personal. There are a few basic rules. All included projects must have the same presentation format. Inconsistencies will be obvious and do not make for a good impression. Vertical or horizontal orientation of individual projects should be consistent throughout the portfolio, especially if it is bound. It is very awkward to keep turning a portfolio horizontally and vertically to orient the project. If the orientation must change, then the project should be removed and displayed for the interviewer.

The reproduction process is very important in creating your portfolio. You should never include your originals, for you may never see them again. Most modern formats, including CAD drawings and scanned illustrations, are the best because they are the cleanest and easily touched up.

PROFESSIONAL REFERENCES

No matter how many good things you say and demonstrate about yourself on your resume or in job interviews, at some point employers are going to want an objective second opinion of you (and probably a third and fourth opinion, as well). That is where your professional references come in.

The time and care you invest in choosing and even coaching the people who will serve as your references might very well determine whether you are ultimately offered the job or internship you so badly want. Most employers are not going to rely on your word alone, no matter how sincere and truthful you might be in marketing yourself for a position. Most employers are not going to rely solely on their own judgments of you, either. They simply have not known you long enough to fully assess you and your education, experience and skills; nor have they seen how you fare under pressure, in stress-filled situations.

Most employers will want to hear from your references in hopes that these people who know you a little better can speak to your skills and personal traits based on their past experiences with you. It goes without saying that the better your references are, the better your chances will be when it comes to landing the position.

While your family and friends may love you and speak highly of you, they are not the best professional references. Instead, approach your current and past employers, professors, advisors and supervisors.

Employers will probably be your best professional references because they can discuss your work habits and the skills you gained on the job. They will also have the most in common with the people who are considering you for the job or internship you are seeking.

If you have gotten to know some of your professors fairly well, ask them to be references for you. While professors may not be able to speak to the skills you gained in an employment setting, they can describe your academic abilities and your skills in areas like research, written communication and oral presentation. Maybe you have worked closely with your student organization's advisor. If so, this person can talk about your leadership skills, your people and teamwork skills and perhaps even your fundraising or member recruitment skills.

Ask each of your references to write you a brief letter that you can give to prospective employers. Make the job easy for the people you select by giving them a list of skills and experiences you would like them to highlight in their letters, as well as a copy of your resume. The more information you can give them, the better; after all, some of them might be writing letters for several or even dozens of applicants.

Once you have your reference letters in hand, ask the people you have chosen if they would be willing to speak to employers directly as well. In most cases, employers will treat reference letters as mere starting points of the reference-checking process; they know that such letters will be glowing with praise for you (otherwise you would not have submitted them). So they will want to contact your references by phone or email to get more specifics about you and your skills and experiences. Your references need to be prepared for those calls or emails.

Finding good references and convincing them to help you can be tricky and time-consuming to be sure, often because the people you approach are simply busy with so many other things. But if you choose your references with care and do all you can to make the process straightforward for them, you will wind up with one, two, three or more people who might serve as that extra edge you need to land the position you want.

THE INTERVIEW

This is the last step. You have researched the company, tailored your cover letter, perfected your resume and organized your portfolio. Now is the hardest part when you have to sell yourself, in person. Everything up to now has been about getting this interview. Now make it worth your while.

Once you have obtained an interview with a firm, it is easy to become nervous. You may want to avoid thinking of the coming experience. This time is important in mentally and academically prepare you for the interview.

Be on time; plan ahead for the correct date, time and location. Make travel arrangements, possibly make a simple run-through. Along with your portfolio, bring extra copies of your resume and references. These items should be easily accessible but discreetly stored until time to exhibit.

Dress appropriately and professionally. If you are unaware of the dress style of the company, ask the receptionist. It can be as bad to overdress as it is to under dress. Be sure your clothes are clean and neatly pressed or steamed. Your hair should likewise be clean and neat. Avoid excessive jewelry and fragrances. When you arrive, make sure to straighten your appearance before checking-in with the receptionist. Try to bring as few possessions into the interview: have a receptionist take your coat, umbrella, etc. Extra articles may become cumbersome. Remove any chewing gum and do not smoke prior to the interview.

When the interviewer arrives, make sure to welcome them with a warm greeting, a bright smile and a firm handshake. Follow the interviewers lead: they will offer you a seat and initiate the conversation. Be relaxed and friendly. Listen to all questions and think through your answers before you respond.

A quick note on illegal questions: it is illegal for an interviewer to ask anything personal that is not directly job-related. Personal questions considered to be job-related usually are allowed in the interview or on the job application. Examples of legal, personal questions include: "Are you ever been convicted of a crime?" and "Can you perform the jobs essential functions with or without reasonable accommodations?"

During the interview, make sure to act your best. Do not accept beverages to diminish possibility of spilling. Be conscious of correct posture. Avoid fidgeting. Use direct eye contact. Avoid using slang. Beware of any nervous habits you might have and avoid them during the interview (i.e. twirling hair, overusing words, jingling change in your pocket, cracking knuckles).

At the conclusion of a job interview you may be asked, "Do you have any questions." An incorrect response would be, "no." This is your opportunity to ask some critical questions, which may help you decide whether you want to work for this company. The first round of interviews is about discovery of the position, not benefits and raises. Good questions to ask in the first round are about the job content and the company's culture and future. The interview should be an exchange of information. What does the company want and what do you offer along with what do you want. It is essential to express an interest in the company and the work being done. By asking questions, you will demonstrate investigative skills; illustrate your interest in the company, and your belief in yourself.

Many companies use phone interviews as an initial employment screening technique because they save companies time and serve as a more realistic screening alternative for cases in considering out-of-town candidates. Preparation for a phone interview is similar to preparing for an in-person interview. Treat the phone interview seriously. Have your resume and cover letter in front of you. Since they cannot see you, make a cheat sheet by jotting down a few critical points you want to make including bulleted skills and experiences. Make sure that you are using a high-quality phone so that the interview has the best possible chance of hearing you. To maintain the correct mental state, it is encouraged to dress up and maintain correct posture during the interview; it will translate in your attitude and vocal quality.

Since one of the top fears is rejection and one of your top needs is acceptance, it is not surprising that interviews make people sweat. The first perspective to remember is that this situation is not intended to inflict pain; it is just a conversation. The worst that could happen is you will not get the job, which may not have been the correct job for you. Secondly, with it being a conversation, it is a two-way process. You are interviewing potential employers and much as they are interviewing you.

Finally, not every job is the right job. It is important to understand the corporate climate before accepting the position. In the zeal and desire to land a new job, many job hunters overlook the "writing on the wall." The evidence is all there: how you are treated during the interviewing process is a key indicator of how you will be treated on the job.

THE FOLLOW-UP LETTER

The thank-you note is a necessary tool for any job-hunting strategy. But should you send it by email or post, handwritten or typed? In this fast-paced climate, the question baffles even the most sophisticated job hunters.

How did the company initially contact you? If you have always corresponded with them via email for setting up the interview and answering questions, then by all means send an email thank-you note as soon as you return from an interview. However, make sure to follow it up with a typed note to show that you are professional. Email thank-you notes have one clear advantage over their 'snail mail' counterpart: they can put your name in front of the interviewer on the same day of your interview. If the company you interviewed with is formal and traditional, use snail mail to send your thank-you note.

Should it be handwritten or typed? Typed is standard. Not only will you show that you are business-like, you will also prove you know how to put together the salutation, format a letter and sign it off. Executives want to know their employees can do this, since writing letters to clients and vendors will be a big part of your job. Handwritten notes are appropriate if you would like to extend your thanks to others in the office who helped you out. For example, if a receptionist, assistant, office manager or other person involved with the interviewing process was especially helpful, then a handwritten note is a nice gesture to show your appreciation.

More important is what to say and how you say it. A standard thank-you note should thank the person for the opportunity to interview with the company. Recap some of the conversational highlights; clarify any information you needed to check on for the interviewer; and most importantly, highlight your skills. Use the last paragraph as the chance to state, "the job is a good fit for me because XYZ, through my past experience in LMNOP." Interviewers have short memories. A thank-you note is your final chance to stand apart from all of the others who want the same position.

THE REJECTION LETTER

You have remained upbeat during the process, hoping to get an offer and instead receive a form letter saying you have not been chosen. You are not alone in you feel let down. Instead of wallowing in self-pity, you can regain power by staying proactive. If you really want to work for a particular company, write a letter stating how disappointed you are that the position went to another candidate, remind them of all the positive traits you could bring to the organization, and let them know you are still very interested in working for the company if something should change or open up. If you felt a positive connection with the interviewer, you might be able to speak with them about the interview and where you fell short. Taking action will make you feel you at least gave it one more shot and will make you feel more in control for having done something positive.

Remember that you were selected above many others and got invited to an interview; and if gotten invited to a second interview even better. Continue to work on your interview skills and rate yourself after each performance. Eventually you will find the right place for you.

GETTING FEEDBACK

Imagine if on your way out of the interview, you were handled a critique of how you did, detailing what went right, what went wrong and how you could improve your skills for the next interview. There is practically no chance that would ever happen. But when you follow up a few days later you can try to gain some sort of feedback. The interviewer will not normally reveal what eliminated you. Most HR departments have policies against giving out interview information because they fear discrimination claims if a candidate misinterprets the feedback; but every once in a while, an interviewer will divulge some useful information.

There are a few rules to follow when asking for feedback: be sure to relay your disappointment in not getting the offer and say that you would be interested in interviewing if anything opens up; politely ask if there is any feedback that would help you improve your chances in your next interview; keep your discussion short; thank the interviewer for the feedback and the chance to improve your skills; and take the advice given and change some of your techniques to improve for your next interview.

FINAL INSPIRATION

In the current job market, you better have your act together or you will not stand a chance against the competition. Remember these ten basic points to lead to your job-hunt success:

1. Look Sharp

2. Be on Time

3. Do Your Research

4. Be Prepared

5. Show Enthusiasm

6. Listen

7. Answer the Question Asked

8. Give Specific Examples

9. Ask Questions

10. Follow Up

It is important to appear confident and cool for the interview. There is no way to predict what an interview holds, but by following these important rules you will feel less anxious and will be ready to positively present yourself.

4

Experience and Examination

THE INTERNSHIP

Internships are becoming widespread today. As an employer, hiring someone right out of college can be somewhat daunting because students lack real-life skills. Having an internship in your pocket makes you stand out from the crowd; which is why many schools are making internships a requirement prior to graduation. Plus, an internship may turn into your first position after graduation.

Whether for pay or on a volunteer basis, the internship provides valuable exposure to on-the-job experience, as well as being an important step in the networking process. By spending time in a job situation and making real-life design decisions, you will gain confidence in yourself and your design ability. The internship often provides your first exposure to office politics and job tactics.

BASIC SKILLS

There are some skills, abilities and habits all employees need to bring to a job. Common traits all employers look for include the following:

Mathematics and English Skills: Most jobs require employees to follow directions or add numbers. Employees should have basic skills in reading, writing and math.

Communication Skills: Almost all jobs require some interaction among workers. Employees must be able to exchange information with their peers, supervisors, and clients.

Consideration and Respect: Employees should display professionalism and courtesy in dealing with their supervisors and coworkers. Employers are more likely to promote those who can work as part of a team and get along well with others.

Willingness to Learn and an Open Mind: Employers hire workers who can accomplish tasks efficiently. Employees should strive to improve existing methods and be willing to learn new techniques and procedures.

YOUR FIRST JOB

As you step into your first post-grad work experience, there are a lot of things you need to know that your textbooks did not teach. Here is what you should be gleaning.

Your first job in no way predicts where you will ultimately end up. Talk to anyone in mid-career and you will be shocked where the career began. Your main task on your first job is to test your wings, learning how organizations work, how business gets done and what makes people and organizations successful. Career (not job) changes are in your future as you learn, grow and change.

One of the biggest complaints about new college grads is that they often expect too much too soon and come across as thinking they know more than seasoned employees. Know that you will need to earn your stripes as well as the trust of colleagues and supervisors before being given more responsibility. Especially watch your attitude with support staff so as not to come across as arrogant or condescending.

Observe how the staff interacts with each other and how things get done. Who really calls the shots, compared with what the organizational chart says? Who seems to have more power than might be indicated by his job title? Who is looked up to, admired and why? Pay attention to the behaviors and results valued in your organization. Also, find out what the company stands for. Ask what the organization's mission statement is and how it is different from the competition. Do you get a feeling of teamwork in operation? What are the written and unwritten rules? What kinds of people seem successful and why?

Your first job is a chance for you to learn more about yourself, what you're good at, what you're not and especially the kind of work you prefer and enjoy. Pay attention to the body language of others as they come in contact with you; this will help you understand how others respond to you. Observe the kinds of people who energize you and alternatively, the types who drain you. Pay attention to the types of management styles that bring out the best in you.

Understand that the new work paradigm is that you, not the organization, are in charge of your career. Gone are the days when the organization takes responsibility for moving you along from first job to retirement. Your task is to make a contribution to the company and develop skills you can take with you when the time comes to leave. What are some good ways to build skills? Volunteer for interesting projects and keep your eyes open for any professional development opportunities both within and outside the organization. Keep a skills portfolio folder, and as you learn, develop or demonstrate a skill, write it down and stick it in that file.

Even if it is not part of the protocol, ask for a three-month and/or a six-month evaluation. Stay on top of how well you are meeting expectations and eliminate any problem areas. Always ask how you can improve your performance. Put any compliments you receive, written or verbal, in a file, including any good work evaluations. You can use these comments for impact in both future cover letters and job interviews.

Internal job postings can be used as a way of understanding the breadth of work done in the organization and other positions that might interest you down the road, either there or at some other company. Pay particular attention to understanding the job requirements.

NETWORKING

Networking is probably the most often used buzzword of the past decade. In fact it is overused. Networking is simply keeping in touch with those who we feel can help us personally or professionally; and keeping in touch with those who we can help as well. It is building a foundation of contacts that can help, advise, friendship, references, guidance, mentoring or information. The people we network with might hear of job opportunities, new products or information that could advance us.

Start the networking process by listing all your personal friends and business associates. Contact them initially by letter, explaining your situation, explaining your career direction and ask for advice and ideas. After sending letters is the follow-up phone call. This is a great step to re-establishing old friendships. Make sure to keep this step very informal and personal; ask about your associate's work, their family and recent events. Make sure to ask for suggestions and other contacts. Remember, you should not feel that this is unfair to your friends; most people have an inert need to help. If you are a shy person, it is better to put yourself in situations where you will have the opportunity to meet people without being outgoing; e.g. volunteer work.

Once your network has been established, expect it to change; it might change in size or content—the important thing is to not let it die. Keep in touch with your group of contacts (network). Sometimes a contact, job opportunity, information or potential project will come from where you least expect. Your responsibility in the network is to be professional, honest, positive and to help others as well. Utilize email, post or even the telephone to follow up with anyone that has helped you—always be sure to thank those who have helped you along your path.

IDEP PROGRAM

The Interior Design Experience Program (IDEP) is a monitored, documented experience program administered by NCIDQ for graduates of interior design education programs. This is a volunteer program and is not mandatory for taking the NCIDQ.

The career path of a professional interior designer involves formal education, entry-level work experience and a qualification examination. Entry-level work is required of candidates for the NCIDQ examination, as well as by the major interior design organizations for professional membership. State and provincial licensing boards require proof of quality interior design experience for licensure and registration. IDEP has been developed to assist entry-level interior designers in obtaining a broad range of quality professional experience and to establish performance guidelines for the work experience of new interior designers. The program serves as the essential transition between formal education and professional practice, recognizing the unique differences between programs of education and diversity of practice.

Most important, IDEP facilitates the development of competent designers who can provide exemplary interior design services and work as members of teams of professionals involved in the design of the built environment.

STEP WORKSHOP

ASID offers a preparatory class for the NCIDQ exam called STEP. The STEP workshop provides participants with the opportunity to experience exams and practicum exercises patterned after the newest NCIDQ format in an environment that affords the opportunity to assess strengths and weaknesses. Through this process, designers can analyze their own skills and adequately assess which areas require further preparation. The workshop, comprised of 20 hours of instruction presented over a 2-1/2 day period, is conducted periodically nation-wide.

Participants are encouraged to have their STEP workshop experience 6 to 12 months prior to taking the NCIDQ exam so that skill areas that require further preparation may be studied. However, the STEP workshop can also be a valuable experience for participants sitting for the exam in less than 6 months.

Anyone wishing to prepare for the NCIDQ exam may take STEP. Practicing educators and designers have been carefully selected and trained to deliver the program. Their interaction with each participant is a valuable part of each work-shop. Although books and study guides do exist and are helpful, they do not take place of an interactive prep course like the STEP workshop

NCIDQ EXAM

The NCIDQ examination is the most effective vehicle for measuring minimum competency in the practice of interior design, with all questions addressing the health, safety and welfare of the public. It is the only interior design exam devel-oped and administered in North America by an agency that is independent from other interior design organizations.

The exam eligibility requirement is a combined minimum of six years of interior design education and actual, full-time interior design experience (neither being less than two years). For complete eligibility requirements, contact NCIDQ. Please note that if you reside in a licensed state or province and intend to become licensed, you must contact the appropriate regulatory agency before completing the NCIDQ to verify local requirements for licensure.

The NCIDQ is a three-part examination format that places a greater emphasis on practical experience. The test is divided into six performance areas and five criti-cal issues that characterize the work of interior design:

Performance Areas:
1.   Project Organization
2.   Programming
3.   Schematics

4. Design Development
5. Contract Documents
6. Contract Administration

Critical Issues:
1. Health and Safety
2. Welfare
3. Function
4. Business, Law and Ethics
5. Design Synthesis

The exam consists of two multiple-choice sections and one practicum section administered over a two-day period.

Section 1: Principles and Practices of Interior Design

Multiple Choice; 150 Questions, 3.5 Hours

Section one addresses the areas of project organization, programming, schematics and design development. This section includes 25 experimental questions that will not be used to determine your score. Some questions incorporate drawings, pictures and symbols typical in the interior design profession, requiring you to recall, apply and analyze information.

Section 2: Contract Development and Administration

Multiple Choice; 125 Questions, Three Hours

Section two addresses the areas of contract documents and contract administration. This section includes 25 experimental questions that will not be used to determine your score but are used to organize future exams. Some questions incorporate drawings, pictures and symbols typical in the interior design profession, requiring you to recall, apply and analyze information.

Section 3: Schematics and Design Development

Practicum; Part 1—Four Hours, Part 2—Three Hours

Section three requires you to produce a design solution. You will receive a program based on a mixed-use facility. All candidates for a given test date will receive the same scenario. All design solutions must address the principals of assessable design.

CONTINUING EDUCATION

Continuing education in interior design emphasizes attitudes, competencies, knowledge and skills in a specific subject with the long-term goal of enhancing an individual participant's performance. Learning experiences focus on the thought, action and reaction skills necessary for interior designers to maintain an advanced level of professionalism. Meanwhile, these experiences fulfill various continuing education units (CEU) requirements for licensure and some professional membership.

Continuing education in interior design is coordinated through the professional development committees of IDCEC (Interior Design Continuing Education Council) and its member organizations, ASID, IDC, IDEC, IIDA, and NKBA.

PROFESSIONAL SUPPORT SYSTEMS

Professional organizations offer many benefits to the designer, some which are immediately recognized and others, which become evident only after a period of time. Some of the benefits and opportunities that a professional organization can offer are continuing education programs, social interaction with your peers and power in numbers to influence legislation and conditions in the marketplace. Two of the main professional interior design organizations worldwide are ASID and IIDA.

The American Society of Interior Designers (ASID) is a non-profit professional society representing the interests of interior designers and the interior design community. With some 30,000 members, ASID, formed in 1975, is the oldest and largest professional organization for interior designers in the U.S., with the largest residential and commercial memberships. The Society is lead by a volunteer board of directors that includes the Society's president, president-elect, and immediate past president. A small staff housed in the Society's headquarters in Washington, D.C carries out daily operations.

The International Interior Design Association (IIDA) is a professional networking and educational association. Founded in 1994, IIDA consists of more than 10,000 members in eight specialty forums, nine regions, and more than 30 chapters around the world committed to enhancing the quality of life through excellence in interior design and advancing interior design through knowledge.

Our Acronymic Vocabulary

AIA	American Institute of Architects
ALCA	Associated Landscape Contractors of America
AFMA	American Furniture Manufacturers Association
AIGA	American Institute of Graphic Arts
APA	American Planning Association
ASME	American Society of Mechanical Engineers
ASID	American Society of Interior Designers
ASLA	American Society of Landscape Architects
AWI	American Woodworkers Institute
BOMA	Building Owners and Managers Association
BIFMA	Business and Institutional Furniture Manufacturers Association
CRI	Carpet and Rug Institute
CSI	Construction Specification Institute
EDRA	Environmental Design Research Association
FIDER	Foundation for Interior Design Educational Research
IALD	International Association of Lighting Designers
IDC	Interior Designers of Canada
IDCEC	Interior Design Continuing Education Council
IDEC	Interior Designers Educators Council
IDSA	Industrial Designers Society of America
IEA	International Ergonomics Association
IEEE	Institute for Electrical and Electronics Engineers
IESNA	Illuminating Engineering Society of North America
IFDA	International Furnishings and Design Association
IFI	International Federation of Interior Architects and Designers
IFMA	International Facility Management Association
IIDA	International Interior Design Association
ISIAQ	International Society of Indoor Air Quality and Climate
ISP	Institute of Store Planners
NAHB	National Association of Home Builders
NARI	National Association of Remodeling Industry
NCIDQ	National Council for Interior Design Qualification
NCQLP	National Council on Qualifications for the Lighting Profession
NEWH	Network of Executive Women in Hospitality
NKBA	National Kitchen and Bath Association
OBD	Organization of Black Designers
USGBC	U.S. Green Building Council

Appendices

APPENDIX: RESOURCES AND CONTACTS

For further information within the United States on interior design degrees, continuing educations, and licensure programs in interior design and interior design research, contact the following organizations.

American Society for Interior Designers
608 Massachusetts Ave, NE
Washington, DC 20002-6006
1 (202) 546-3480
www.asid.org

Foundation for Interior Design Education Research
146 Monroe Ctr NW, Ste 1318
Grand Rapids, MI 49503-2822
1 (616) 458-0400
www.fider.org

Industrial Designers Society of America
45195 Business Court, Ste 250
Dulles, VA 20166
1 (703) 707-6000
www.idsa.org

Institute of Store Planners
25 N Broadway
Tarrytown, NY 10591-3221
1 (800) 379-9912
www.ispo.org

Interior Design Educators Council
7150 Winton Dr, Ste 300
Indianapolis, IN 46268-4398
1 (317) 328-4437
www.idec.org

International Interior Design Association
13-122 Merchandise Mart
Chicago, IL 60654-1104

1 (312) 467-1950
www.iida.org

National Council for Interior Design Qualification
1200 18th St NW Ste 1001
Washington, DC 20036-2506
www.ncidq.org

Organization of Black Designers
300 M Street, SW, Ste N110
Washington, DC 20024-4019
1 (202) 659-3918
www.core77.com/obd

APPENDIX: INTERVIEW CHECKLIST

Use this checklist to keep you focused before, during and after the interview. Creating a cheat sheet will help you feel more prepared and confident. You should not memorize that is on the sheet or check it off during the interview. Your cheat sheet is created to help remind you of key facts.

In the Days before the Interview

1. Draw a line down the center of a piece of paper. On the left side, make a bulleted list of what the employer is looking for based on the job posting. On the right side make a bulleted list of the qualities you possess that fit those requirements.

2. Research the company, the industry and the competition.

3. Prepare your 60-second personal statement: "Tell me about yourself," question.

4. Write at least five success stories to answer behavioral interview questions ("Tell me about a time when…" or "Give me an example of the time…").

5. List ten questions to ask the interviewer about the job, the company and the industry.

6. Research salary and determine your worth.

7. Determine your salary needs based on your living expenses: what is your bottom line?

8. Get permission from your references to use their names.

Before You Go to the Interview

1. Do you look professional? Check yourself in the mirror; part of your confidence will come from looking good.

2. Carry these items to the interview:

   Several copies of your resume on quality paper

   A copy of your references

   A pad of paper on which to take notes

Directions to the interview site

3. Prepare answers to the ten most common interview questions:

   Tell me about yourself.

   Why did you leave or why are you leaving your last position?

   What do you know about this company?

   What are your goals?

   What are your strengths and weaknesses?

   Why do you want to work for this company?

   What has been your most significant achievement?

   How would your last boss and colleagues describe you?

   Why should we hire you?

   What are your salary expectations?

Upon Arrival

1. Arrive early. Enter the building ten minutes before your interview.

2. Review your prepared stories and answers.

3. Go to the restroom and check your appearance one last time.

4. Announce yourself to the receptionist in a professional manner.

5. Stand and greet your interviewer with a hearty handshake.

6. Smile and look into the interviewer's eyes.

During the Interview

1. Try to focus on the points you have prepared without sounding rehearsed or stiff.

2. Relax and enjoy the conversation. Learn what you can about the company.

3. Ask questions and listen; read between the lines.

4. At the conclusion, thank the interviewer and determine the next steps.

5. Ask for the interviewer's business card so you can send a follow-up letter.

After the Interview

1. As soon as possible, write down what you are thinking and feeling.

2. Later in the day, look at what you wrote and assess how you did.

3. Write a follow-up thank-you letter, reminding the interviewer of your qualities.

APPENDIX: STATE REGISTRATION LAWS

This listing is current as of January 2004.

For the most current information, contact your local regulatory agency. A listing of these agencies can be found online at www.ncidq.org/licens.html.

Legend:
Type of Act
Required Education and Experience
Regulating State Board/Agency

ALABAMA

Title/Practice Interior Designer/Registered Interior Designer
Education: 60 quarters or 48 tri semester credit hours/4 years for the registered level. Total Education Plus Experience: 6 years

Alabama State Board of Registration for Interior Design:
Post Office Box 11026
Birmingham, AL 35202
Phone—(205) 879-6785

ARKANSAS

Title Registered Interior Designer
Education: 2 years (min. 4 years educ.4 yrs. after enactment) Total Education
Experience: 6 years

Arkansas Board of Registered Interior Designers
Post Office Box 250220
Little Rock, AR 72225-0220
Phone—(870) 226-6875

CALIFORNIA

Self-Certification Title Certified Interior Designer
Education: None. Total Education
Experience: 6-8 years depending on education

California Council for Interior Design Certification (CCIDC)
1605 Grand Avenue, Suite #4
San Marcos, CA 92069-2440
Phone—(760) 761-4734

COLORADO

Permitting Statute
Education: 2 years. Total Education Plus Experience: 6 years

CONNECTICUT

Title Interior Designer

Connecticut Department of Consumer Protection
Professional Licensing Div.—Interior Design
165 Capitol Avenue
Hartford, Connecticut 06106
Phone—(860) 713-6135

DISTRICT OF COLUMBIA

Title/Practice Interior Designer
Education: 2 years (as required by NCIDQ to take exam)
Total Education Plus Experience: 6 years

DC Department of Consumer and Regulatory Affairs
C/O DC Board of Architecture and Interior Design
941 N. Capitol Street NE, Room 7200
Washington, DC 20002
Phone—(202) 442-4330

FLORIDA

Title/Practice Interior Designer
Education: 2 years. Total Education Plus Experience: 6 years

Florida Board of Architecture and Interior Design
Northwood Center

1940 N. Monroe St., Suite 60
Tallahassee, Florida 32399-0751
Phone—(850) 487-1395

GEORGIA

Title Registered Interior Designer
Education: 4 years or first professional degree
Total Education Plus Experience: 4 years (no experience specified)

Georgia State Board of Architects and Interior Designers
Barbara Kitchens, Exec. Director
237 Coliseum Drive
Atlanta, GA 31217-3858
Phone—(478) 207-1400

ILLINOIS

Title Interior Designer/Registered Interior Designer
Education: 2 years. Total Education Plus Experience: 6 years

Illinois Department of Professional Regulations
Post Office Box 7007
Springfield, IL 62791
Phone—(217) 785-0813

KENTUCKY

Title/Certified Interior Designer

Kentucky State Board of Examiners and Registration of Architects
301 East Main Street, Ste. 860
Lexington, KY 40507
Phone—(859) 246-2069

LOUISIANA

Title/Practice Registered Interior Designer
Education: 2 years. Total Education Plus Experience: 6 years

Louisiana State Board of Examiners of Interior Design
2900 Westfork, Ste. 200
Baton Rouge, Louisiana 70827
Phone—(225) 298-1283

MAINE

Title Certified Interior Designer
Education: 4 years. Total Education Plus Experience: 6 years

Maine State Board for Licensure of Architects, Landscape Architects and Interior Designers
State House Station #35
Augusta, ME 04333
Phone—(207) 624-8603

MARYLAND

Title Certified Interior Designer
Education: 4 years. Total Education Plus Experience: 6 years

Maryland Department of Licensing and Regulation
Board of Certified Interior Designers
500 N. Calvert St.
Rm. 308
Baltimore, MD 21202
Phone—(410) 230-6322

MINNESOTA

Title Certified Interior Designer
Education: Board determined.
Total Education Plus Experience: 6 years

Minnesota AELSLAGID
Office of the Board
133 7th Street East
St. Paul, MN 55101-2333
Phone—(651) 296-2388

MISSOURI

Title Registered Commercial Interior Designer
Education: 2 years. Total Education Plus Experience: 6 years

Missouri Interior Design Council
Post Office Box 1335
Jefferson City, MO 65102-1335
Phone—(573) 522-4683

NEVADA

Title/Practice Registered Interior Designer
Education: 4 years. Total Education Plus Experience: 6 years

Nevada Board of Architecture, Interior Design & Residential Design
2080 E. Flamingo Rd., Ste. 225
Las Vegas, NV 89119
Phone—(702) 486-7300

NEW JERSEY

Title
Education: 2 years. Total Education Plus Experience: 6 years

New Jersey State Board of Architects
P.O. Box 45001
Newark, N.J. 07101
Phone—(973) 504-6385

NEW MEXICO

Title Interior Designer
Education: 2 years. Total Education Plus Experience: 6 years

New Mexico Board of Interior Design
Post Office Box 25101
Santa Fe, New Mexico 87504
Phone—(505) 476-7077

NEW YORK

Title Certified Interior Designer
Education: 2 years. Total Education Plus Experience: 7 years

New York State Education Dept.
Board of Interior Design
Cultural Education Center, Room 3019
Empire State Plaza
Albany, NY 12230
Phone—(518) 474-3846

PUERTO RICO

Title/Practice Interior Designer/Interior Decorator
Education: 2 years or 480 hours
Total Education Plus Experience: 2 years (no experience specified)

Puerto Rico State Department
Examining Board of Interior Designers
Post Office Box 3271
San Juan, Puerto Rico 00902
Phone—(787) 722-2122

TENNESSEE

Title Registered Interior Designer
Education: 2 years. Total Education Plus Experience: 6 years

Tennessee Dept. of Commerce & Insurance
Board of Architectural & Engineering Examiners
3rd Floor Volunteer Plaza Building
500 James Robertson Parkway
Nashville, TN 37243-1142
Phone—(615) 741-3221

TEXAS

Title Interior Designer
Education: 1 year.
Total Education Plus Experience: 5-6 years depending on education

Texas Board of Architectural Examiners
Post Office Box 12337
Austin, TX 78711-2337
Phone—(512) 305-8539

VIRGINIA

Title Certified Interior Designer
Education: 4 years. Total Education Plus Experience: 6 years

Virginia APELSCIDLA Board
3600 W. Broad St.
Richmond, VA 23230-4917
Phone—(804) 367-851

WISCONSIN

Title Wisconsin Registered Interior Designer
Education: 2 years. Total Education Plus Experience: 6 years

Wisconsin Department of Regulation & Licensing
Post Office Box 8935
Madison, WI 53708
Phone—(608) 266-5439

0-595-31909-2

Printed in the United States
46059LVS00004B/75